Aircraft

WHITE STAR PUBLISHERS

CONTENTS

TEXT
RICCARDO NICCOLI

GRAPHIC DESIGN
PAOLA PIACCO

1 A Fiat CR.42 biplane fighter of the 4th Squadron of the Italian Royal Air Force photographed at the airfield of El Adem, in Libya, in 1940.

2-3 The Italian air acrobatics team, the "Frecce Tricolori," has flown with Alenia Aermacchi MB-339 trainers since 1982.

INTRODUCTION

As is well known, the history of human flight is in part the story of the realization of a dream: to be able to fly free in the sky, overcome the force of gravity and move about at will, hovering high in the heavenly vault to take in the earth at a glance, or to descend and race along close to the ground to taste the thrill of speed. All this was only possible thanks to the advent of the motorized vehicle that was heavier than air, a means of transport controlled by man's will: the airplane.

For about 110 years, thanks to the plane, man has not only fulfilled his dream of freedom, but has also improved the lives of his peers and helped them, because, thanks to technological progress, the plane has now become not only an instrument of defense and attack, but also a means of transport, and a valuable and sometimes irreplaceable element for saving lives as an emergency ambulance, in search and

4 The Ryan "Spirit of St. Louis" used by Lindbergh was a prototype specially built to set a record.

5 Two French Rafale fighters photographed during an acrobatic maneuver. This is a sophisticated multirole aircraft.

rescue, in creating humanitarian air bridges and in environmental, geographical, hydrological, zoological and archaeological monitoring, both on land and at sea.

With the advent of increasingly modern and advanced aircraft, many international crises have been resolved almost entirely thanks to intervention from the sky, limiting loss of life as far as possible, but, above all, the world has become smaller thanks

sion, travel and contacts between peoples are now the norm, and contribute to the development and prosperity of economies as well as to enhancing peace in the world, increasing our awareness that we are all, deep down, one people who together share the planet earth.

Condensing into these few pages all the airplanes that have contributed to the history of flight would be an impossible task. We will thus limit ourselves to mentioning only the most famous and significant models and the most important events, leaving out other aircraft, such as helicopters, gliders and dirigibles, and also the new UAV, unmanned aircraft, because although useful tools for the purposes ascribed to them, essentially, they do not have anything to do with man's dream of flying.

to our ability to travel in just a few hours to any point on the globe, at competitive prices and with a level of safety that was once unimaginable. In a world that has been globalized by computers and televi-

Chapter 1

THE PIONEERS
OF AVIATION

THE FIRST AIRCRAFT TO CONTRIBUTE TO THE HISTORY OF AVIATION WAS UNDOUBTEDLY THE WRIGHT FLYER, THE FIRST HEAVIER-THAN-AIR AIRCRAFT IN THE WORLD TO EMBARK ON A POWERED, PILOT-CONTROLLED, SUSTAINED FLIGHT. THE HISTORIC EVENT TOOK PLACE AMONG THE DUNES OF KILL DEVIL HILL NEAR KITTY HAWK IN NORTH CAROLINA ON DECEMBER 17, 1903. THE WORK OF THE PIONEERS OF FLIGHT CONTINUED SUCCESSFULLY OVER THE FOLLOWING YEARS, BUT IT WAS ONLY WITH THE OUTBREAK OF THE FIRST WORLD WAR THAT AVIATION HAD THE OPPORTUNITY TO TAKE A REAL LEAP FORWARD, BOTH FROM THE TECHNICAL POINT OF VIEW AS WELL AS FROM A QUANTITATIVE ONE. AT THE BEGINNING OF THE CONFLICT, THE FEW AIRCRAFT IN SERVICE WERE UNARMED AND LARGELY BASED ON SPORTS MODELS. THE WAR, THOUGH, SAW THE BIRTH OF DIFFERENT TYPES SUCH AS FIGHTERS, BOMBERS AND RECONNAISSANCE PLANES, AS WELL AS A BRANCH OF THE ARMED FORCES DEDICATED TO USING THE NEW CRAFT: THE AIR FORCE.

10
The first flight by a motorized aircraft was that of the Wright Brothers, at Kitty Hawk, in North Carolina, on December 17, 1903.

12-13
The German Albatros D.V was one of the best fighter planes of the First World War.

In the years between 1914 and 1918 the principal belligerents produced over 220,000 airplanes; among these, the most important fighters were the French Nieuport 11 and 17, the SPAD S.VII and S.XIII, the German Albatros D.V, Fokker E.III, Dr.I and D.VII, the British Sopwith F1 Camel and RAF S.E.5; the bombers the French Caudron G.4 and Farman F.40, the Italian Caproni Ca.32, the British Vickers Vimy and Handley Page V/1500.

13 top
Nieuport, a French company,
made the model 11 in 1914.

13 bottom
The British Sopwith Camel, of which
about 5500 were built, flew for the first
time 1916 and was an excellent fighter.

L'AFRIQUE DU NORD PAR AVION

AEROPOSTALE

éditions STEP Paris

Siège Social :
92, Avenue des Champs-Élysées
Tél. : Élysées 52-03 - 52-04 - 52-05
Paris VIII°

14
After the First World War, planes were
widely used for transporting mail.

15
The spread of flying was helped by the
organization of a large number of air
shows, such as that in Nice in 1910.

After the war, aviation became a reality that was within the grasp of many. After demobilization, thousands of pilots wanted to continue flying, and tens of thousands of aircraft were sold off by the armed forces. Thus were born, from the "recycling" of war materials, the first airmail services and the first companies for the transport of passengers and goods. The airplane, moreover, proved to be ideal for overcoming the destruction of the war (especially affecting railway lines and bridges) and connecting locations separated by natural obstacles, such as Paris and London. As early as 1919, the first air transport companies appeared in France, Great Britain, Holland, Belgium and Germany. The same era also saw the great raids and explorations, such as the first non-stop flight from Paris to New York, which was undertaken in May 1927 by Charles Lindbergh in a Ryan NYP and completed in a little over 33 hours.

The first commercial airplanes were obviously military aircraft, bombers or single-engine two-seaters, adapted as best they could be, such as the Vickers Vimy Commercial or the Farman F.60. Soon, however, the first aircraft specifically designed to carry passengers began to appear.

The first was the Junkers F13 of 1919, a metal single-engine monoplane that

16
Lindbergh's solo transatlantic flight inspired mass enthusiasm throughout the world. Here he is arriving in Boston.

17
Charles Lindbergh's solo transatlantic flight, in 1927, was an epic undertaking that had a huge impact.

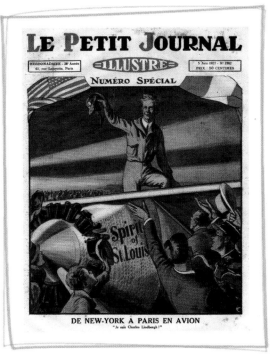

LE PETIT JOURNAL

ILLUSTRE

NUMÉRO SPÉCIAL

DE NEW-YORK À PARIS EN AVION

carried just four passengers, but was still a major success and 350 were built. Then there were the Fokker F.VII for ten passengers, which appeared in 1924, and the Ford Tri-Motor of 1926. With the passing of the Kelly Act in 1925, air transport also began to spread successfully in the United States, to the extent that in a just few years passenger numbers in America exceeded those in Europe.

18
The Boeing 314 Clipper was probably the most famous and efficient
passenger seaplane of its time.

19
The Schneider Trophy was a speed competition for seaplanes,
which promoted technical developments in flight.

In the twenties, the idea began to take hold that the future of air transport, especially long-haul, lay in seaplanes. These aircraft enjoyed great fame
thanks to the establishment of the Schneider Trophy, a race of pure speed,
and the carrying out of a number of raids, such as those made by the Italian
Air Force using the Savoia Marchetti S.55. Large transport seaplanes were the
Donier J Wal and Wal Do X, the Boeing 314 Clipper and Sikorsky S-42, but following the technical developments that took place during the Second World
War, it became evident that the seaplanes, which were too slow and heavy,
would not be the aircraft of the future.

THE SCHNEIDER TROPHY
SEPT. 12TH CONTEST – 1931 –

THE ROYAL AERO CLUB
OFFICIAL
SOUVENIR PROGRAMME

6D.

Printed and published by GALE & POLDEN LTD., LONDON, ALDERSHOT & PORTSMOUTH.

The Handley Page HP.42 appeared in 1932, at the time was the largest land transport aircraft, which could carry up to 38 passengers. The Junkers Ju-52 of 1930 began life as a single-engine craft, but only became a success two years later with the manufacture of a three-engined version, which would also become the most widely used transport aircraft of the Luftwaffe during the Second World War. The de Havilland Dragon also made its debut in 1932, a twin-engined biplane for six passengers which was very successful, and was built in several versions. In the United States the success of airline companies was in part the result of the birth of modern commercial transport aircraft. The earliest was the Boeing 247, of 1933, the first to be entirely made of metal and equipped with a low cantilevered wing, retractable landing gear, engines half-buried in the wings, and deicing systems for the leading edges of the wings and tail. This airplane was able to carry ten passengers for a distance of 745 miles (1,200 km) at a cruising speed of 186 mph (300 km/h).

20-21
The Junkers Ju 52 was the most famous German transport plane in civil and military use in the 1930s and 40s.

The Boeing craft was excellent, but did not carry enough passengers. It was soon superseded by another plane that would forever remain one of the protagonists of aviation history: the Douglas DC-3. This plane was born in 1933 as the DC-1, and carried 12 passengers. The turning point came with the extended DST model, which was created to house 14 sleeping berths in a wider fuselage, but which could also hold up to 21 seats. With this configuration, the aircraft was named the DC-3 in 1936, and it was highly advanced for its time, also coming with a hydraulically retractable undercarriage, variable pitch pro-pellers, flaps to reduce takeoff and landing speed, and improved wings. With the out-break of the Second World War, the DC-3 was developed in a military version, under the name of the C-47 Skytrain (the Dakota for the British RAF) and was used on all fronts, making a significant contribution to the final victory of the Allies. In total, more than 16,000 units of this aircraft were built.

22-23
The Douglas DC-3, called the Dakota in Britain, was the first truly modern transport plane and over 16,000 of them were built.

Chapter 2

THE SECOND WORLD WAR AIRPLANES

As had happened a quarter of a century earlier, so too did the events of the Second World War help to accelerate considerably the technological and technical progress. The planes at the cutting edge were the fighters. The most famous were undoubtedly the British Hawker Hurricane, Supermarine Spitfire and Hawker Typhoon; the American Grumman F6 Hellcat, Vought F4 Corsair, Republic P-47 Thunderbolt and North American P-51 Mustang; the German Messerschmitt Bf 109 and Me 262, and Focke-Wulf Fw190; the Soviet Yakovlev and Yak-9, and Lavochkin La-5; the Italian Macchi MC.202 and Fiat CR.42; and the Japanese Mitsubishi Zero and Nakajima Ki-43.

The Hurricane flew for the first time in 1935, but in 1940, it could no longer be considered a modern fighter. All the same, this was the plane that faced up to the initial attack of the Luftwaffe, and helped Britain resist, while the new Spitfire was produced in sufficient quantities to deal with the demands of wartime. The Typhoon, born in 1940 as the successor to the Hurricane, proved to be an excellent ground-attack airplane, and in 1943 it gave birth to the Tempest.

24
At the outbreak of the Battle of Britain, in 1940, the Hawker Hurricane was in use at 32 RAF squadrons.

26-27
A formation of six Mk I Spitfires photographed
flying during the Battle of Britain, in 1940.

27
The Typhoon was armed with four 0.7 in
(20 mm) cannon, and could carry bombs
or rockets for ground attack.

472218

28-29
The best fighter introduced by the United States in the Second World War was the North American P-51, shown here in the D version.

29
The Soviet Yak-9, developed in 1942, was an excellent multirole fighter and almost 17,000 were built.

The whole of aviation made great progress, moreover, in the field of engines, navigation systems, aerodynamics and electronics, which began to make its appearance with the first radar systems and devices for jamming enemy equipment.

Other important aircraft of the period

were the British Avro Lancaster bomber, the American Consolidated B-24 Liberator, Boeing B-17 Flying Fortress and B-29 Superfortress, and the German Heinkel He 111, the German dive bomber Junkers Ju 87 Stuka and the Soviet Ilyushin Il-2 Sturmovik.

30
The protagonist of hundreds of night raids on Germany, the RAF Avro Lancaster.

30-31
The most famous heavy bomber in the Second World War was the Boeing B-17.

During the 1940s the most evident progress was that relating to the system of propulsion, given that the research carried out in Great Britain and Germany led to the building of jet engines that were increasingly reliable and powerful. The first aircraft truly powered by a jet engine was the Heinkel He 178, which took off in August 1939. Within a few years it became clear that the future of high-performance flight would come from these engines, which were developed as a priority in the United States and the Soviet Union as well, also thanks to the acquisition of the enormous amount of

technical material and researchers who transferred from Germany to the two victorious countries. The first mass-produced jet aircraft was the Messerschmitt Me 262, which flew for the first time in July 1942. It was followed by the British Gloster Meteor in 1943 and the Lockheed P-80 in 1944.

32-33
The Messerschmitt Me 262 was the first jet fighter in history and was also adapted for night-fighting, attack and reconnaissance missions.

34 top
The U.S. Republic F-84 was one of the first successful jet fighter-bombers.

34 bottom
The first true Soviet jet fighter was the MiG-15, which appeared in 1947.

35
A protagonist of the Korean War, the North American F-86 Sabre
was the best fighter aircraft of the early 1950s.

Immediately after the war many new models appeared on the scene, inspired in large part by research conducted in Germany. The first jet fighters of a certain effectiveness were however the American Republic F-84 Thunderjet and Grumman F9 Panther and the Soviet MiG-15. These fighters were the protagonists of the Korean War, which broke out in 1950. The most famous plane of this conflict, though, was the North American F-86 Sabre, the best Western fighter of the war, which managed to get the better of the formidable MiG-15s deployed by the Communist forces.

In the 1950s and 60s, as a result of the tension arising from the East-West stand-off, stemming from the Cold War, technological progress in military aviation was frenetic and echoed in the civil sphere. In October 1947, the Bell X-1 experimental aircraft, piloted by Captain Charles "Chuck" Yeager reached a speed of Mach 1.06 (700 mph - 1127 km/h), breaking the sound barrier in level flight for the first time. Just six years later, the X-1A exceeded Mach 2, while in 1956 this result was achieved for the first time by a production model aircraft, the Lockheed F-104A Starfighter. The most noticeable improvements were in the fields of aerodynamics and propulsion, although significant progress was also achieved in the fields of radar and armaments. The Americans produced the "Century Series" fighters: North American F-100, McDonnell F-101, Convair F-102 and F-106, Lockheed F-104 and Republic F-105 for the Air Force, while the Navy employed aircraft such as the Grumman F-11 Tiger and the Vought F-8 Crusader. A further step forward came with the appearance of the McDonnell Douglas F-4 Phantom II, a large twin-engined plane capable of Mach 2, which flew for the first time in 1958, and could be used as an interceptor, as well as a fighter-bomber and reconnaissance aircraft. In the Soviet Union, the production of fighters was largely entrusted to the technical department at MiG, which produced the MiG-17, MiG-19 and, in 1958, MiG-21, a Mach-2 interceptor that was the basis for many increasingly good models, up to the MiG-21Bis of 1972. The successor to the MiG-21 was the MiG-23, but this was not as successful in export terms.

36
The Lockheed F-104 Starfighter was the first Mach 2 fighter in history.

37
A formation of F-104 Starfighters in flight.

During the Cold War, the arms race did not involve only fighters, but rather – and perhaps more – bombers, as carriers of nuclear weapons, and reconnaissance aircraft. Among these aircraft the most famous were undoubtedly the American Boeing B-47 Stratojet and Boeing B-52 Stratofortress and the Soviet Tupolev Tu-16, Tu-20 and Tu-22, as well as the Lockheed U-2 and SR-71 Blackbird reconnaissance aircraft.

38-39
The famous Boeing B-52, photographed here during in-flight refueling, first flew in 1952, and is still in service today.

39
The legendary Lockheed SR-71 Blackbird strategic reconnaissance aircraft, from 1962, with its 2000 mph (3220 km/h), was the fastest mass-produced aircraft in the world.

40
A Swedish SAAB SK 35C Draken.

Numerous jet aircraft of the new generation were also built in Europe, such as the French Dassault Mystère and Mirage III and 5, the British Hawker Hunter, English Electric Lightning and Hawker Harrier (the first aircraft to take off and land vertically), the Franco-British Jaguar, the Swedish SAAB Draken and Viggen and the Italian FIAT G.91.

41 top
The British Hawker Hunter fighter first flew in 1951, and was successfully used by about 20 countries around the world.

41 bottom
A Dassault Mirage 2000N takes off.

42 top
The Cessna 150/152 was an enormous
success in the field of private flying.

42 bottom
The PA-31 Navajo flew for the first time
in 1964 (under the name of Inca).

42-43
On of the most famous private aircraft
of all time is the Piper PA-18.

Commercial aviation also benefited from technical progress achieved in the military field and the phenomenon of private flying was established. Aircraft clubs became widespread, especially in Europe and North America. Light aircraft circulated among individuals and flight schools of a sort that was within the reach of all, such as the famous Piper J-3 Cub and PA-18, the Piper PA-28 Cherokee, the Beechcraft Bonanza, and the

Cessna 150 and 172. At a higher level, we find the twin-engined leisure craft, such as the Piper PA-23 Apache, PA-31 Navajo and PA-34 Seneca, the Beechcraft Queen and King Air, and the Cessna 400 series, as well as the original 337 Super Skymaster with its "push-pull" formula. The sixties also saw the spread of business jets, such as the first Cessna Citation and Dassault Mystère 20, then renamed as the Falcon 20.

Chapter 3

MODERN MILITARY AIRCRAFT: AT THE EDGE OF TECHNOLOGY

THE MODERN ERA OF MILITARY AIRCRAFT CAN BE CONSIDERED TO HAVE BEGUN IN THE 1970S WITH THE APPEARANCE OF FIGHTER AIRCRAFT THAT REPRESENTED A CLEAR BREAK WITH THE PAST, BOTH WITH REGARD TO TECHNOLOGICAL ASPECTS, AS WELL AS FROM THE POINT OF VIEW OF PERFORMANCE AND OPERATIONAL CAPACITIES. THE INNOVATIONS IN THE MILITARY FIELD IN THAT DECADE INVOLVED THE INTRODUCTION OF ELECTRONIC FLIGHT COMMANDS (FLY-BY-WIRE) CONTROLLED BY COMPUTER, AERODYNAMIC RESEARCH TO REACH PRE-VIOUSLY UNIMAGINABLE LEVELS OF MANEUVERABILITY, INCREASINGLY SOPHISTICATED EQUIPMENT, DOMINATED BY MULTI-FUNCTION SCREENS, HEAD-UP DISPLAY VISORS, AND MULTI-FUNCTION COMMANDS (HOTAS - HANDS ON AND THROTTLE STICK, THAT IS, THE AIRCRAFT CAN BE FLOWN IN COMBAT WITHOUT MOVING THE HANDS FROM THE JOYSTICK AND THE THROTTLE) UP TO THE DEVELOPMENT OF TURBOFAN ENGINES THAT ARE MUCH LIGHTER, MORE POWERFUL AND MORE EFFICIENT THAN PREVIOUS TURBOJETS.

44
A Boeing F-15 Eagle firing an AIM-7 Sparrow missile. This fighter has been in service with the US Air Force since 1975.

46
The attack version of the F-15 is the F-15E Strike Eagle, which entered service in 1988 and is still being produced today for export.

47
The Grumman F-14 Tomcat, which entered service in 1972, was the first aircraft-carrier fighter with variable-sweep wings.

The first of these new aircraft was the Grumman F-14 Tomcat, character-ized by its variable-sweep wings, engines that were far apart from each other, combined with dual tail fins, and very powerful radar coupled with long-range radar-guided missiles. Only two years younger was the McDonnell Douglas (now Boeing) F-15 Eagle, which made its debut in 1972 and proved from the outset to be a fighter pilot's dream, boasting exceptional characteristics from all points of view and, for the first time, a higher thrust than weight ratio in fighting conditions. The project proved to be so successful that, in the mid-1980s, starting from the two-seat model, the F-15E Strike Eagle was built, a multi-role fighter-bomber that delivered impressive performance.

48
An F-16C of Vermont US Air National Guard.

48-49
The US Navy fighter currently in service
is the F/A-18E/F Super Hornet.

Another result of the needs of the U.S. Air Force, which required a lightweight fighter-bomber, was the General Dynamics (now Lockheed Martin) F-16 Fighting Falcon, which flew for the first time in 1974. This aircraft introduced new aerodynamic shapes, especially with regard to the air intake of

the engine, in a ventral position under the nose, and the wing which had a marked junction with the fuselage (Leading Edge Root Extension, or LERX) , which was intended to improve maneuverability and lift. The pilot

sat on a seat inclined 30 degrees backwards to allow a better absorption of the gravity that develops in combat, up to the incredible value of 9 g. To provide better control, the joystick was moved to the right-hand console, and, to

ensure better visibility, the canopy was a single-piece bubble. Last in the U.S. "teen" series was the McDonnell Douglas/Northrop (now Boeing) F/A-18 Hornet, which made its maiden flight in 1978. In 1992, based on the Hornet, the F/A-18E/F Super Hornet was born, an aircraft designed to replace the F-14 and the older F/A-18 models with a low-risk and relatively low-cost solution. The first Super Hornet flew in 1995 and the aircraft entered service in 1999.

50
The French Dassault Mirage 2000 fighter flew for the first time in 1978.

51
The European Panavia Tornado fighter-bomber, here in the markings
of the Luftwaffe, of which almost 1000 have been built.

Across the ocean, in Europe, the aviation industry and governments were not

just standing around watching. France developed a project for a new aircraft in the

Mirage series, which reintroduced the delta wing, which had been so successful

for the Dassault company, but developed more effectively with the introduction

of fly-by-wire flight commands linked with computers, and a new more powerful

turbofan engine. The Mirage 2000 took off in 1978, and the aircraft soon proved

to be a success, being adopted in large numbers by the French Air Force (also

in its attack versions Mirage 2000D and N). To produce a modern and sophisti-

cated attack fighter-bomber, the governments of Italy, Germany and Great Britain

decided instead to pool their resources, creating the Panavia consortium in 1969,

which built the Tornado aircraft, whose first flight took place in 1974.

The Tornado was developed in IDS attack, ADV air defense, and ECR anti-radar attack versions.

On the other side of what was known as the "Iron Curtain," in the Soviet Union, during these years great efforts were being made to try to produce aircraft to match those of the West. In 1977 the prototype of the MiG-29 flew for the first time, an airplane that appeared to be influenced by the most recent U.S. research, but

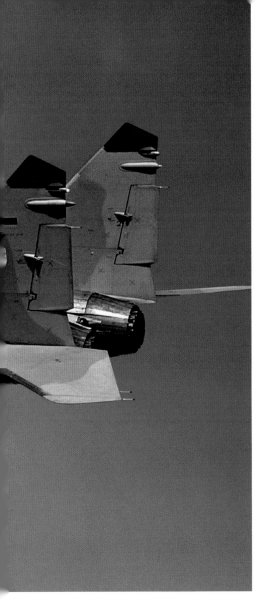

of the other large maker of Soviet fighter aircraft, Sukhoi, which in 1977 flew the first example of the Su-27. This aircraft boasted a large size, an aerodynamic shape similar to that of the F-15, powerful engines and great autonomy. Thanks to these characteristics, the Su-27 from the outset proved to be a great interceptor, but also an excellent basis for the development of increasingly sophisticated and capable models, such as the Su-27K for aircraft carriers, the Su-30, a multi-role two-seater, the two-seater Su-34 long-range bomber and the Su-35 fighter.

which retained its own distinctive appearance, using two turbofan engines at a distance from each other, double fins in the tail, air vents in a ventral position, and LERX surfaces. Much more powerful and capable instead was the product

52-53
One of the most successful modern Soviet fighters is the MiG-29.

53
600 fighters of the Sukhoi Su-27/30 family were produced.

As well as fighters, other types of military aircraft dominated this period. Among the transport aircraft we recall the American Lockheed C-130 Hercules, C-141 Starlifter and C-5 Galaxy, as well as the Franco-German C-160 Transall and the Soviet Ilyushin Il-76, Antonov An-26 and An-124, at the time the largest aircraft in the world. Among the refueling aircraft we cannot forget the Boeing KC-135 Stratotanker, and the McDonnell Douglas KC-10 Extender. Among the trainers the BAE Hawk and Aermacchi MB.339. Among the radar aircraft the Boeing E-3 AWACS and the Ilyushin A-50.

54-55
The biggest transport plane of the
US Air Force is the Lockheed C-5 Galaxy,
capable of transporting more than
100 tons of cargo.

55 bottom
The Soviet Antonov An-26 transport plane
flew for the first time in 1969, and over 1500
were produced in more than 50 countries.

Technological development has obviously not come to a halt, and in more recent years new capabilities have appeared, integrated into more modern aircraft. These relate to the stealth feature, as well as increasingly marked improvements in electronics, and optical, optronic and laser systems capable of allowing identification in night vision and low-light conditions. The aircraft have become increasingly easy to fly and more complex to manage. In this scenario, among the planes that stand out are the Lockheed Martin F-117 Nighthawk, the first stealth fighter-bomber, the Northrop B-2 Spirit, the first stealth bomber with an aerodynamic flying wing design, and the Lockheed Martin F-22 Raptor, the American latest-generation superfighter capable of cruising at supersonic speed, being stealth, and having highly advanced sensors.

56-57
A pair of F-22As of the 1st Fighter Wing of the USAF. This extremely expensive superfighter entered service in 2003.

Europe instead saw the appearance of multi-role fighter aircraft such as the Eurofighter EF.2000 Typhoon, Dassault Rafale and JAS 39 Gripen. China is also starting to feature in the world of high-technology aeronautics, producing projects of their own design after several aircraft built under license. In this way appeared the JF-17 fighter, Chengdu J-10 and the last, the advanced Chengdu J-20 and J-31,

which are in the category of the American F-22 and F-35, as well as the future Russian fighter, the Sukhoi Su-50, which flew for the first time in 2010. The United States has instead created the Joint Strike Fighter

(JSF) program, won by Lockheed Martin with the F-35 project. This plane is characterized by its adoption of many innovative solutions for both on-board systems and for its electronic architecture, and

was developed in three very similar versions: the A for conventional use, the B for short takeoff and vertical landing, and the C for use on conventional aircraft carriers.

58
The Sukhoi T-50 is the prototype of the future superfighter of the Russian Air Force.

58-59
The most modern fighter of the French Air Force today is the Dassault Rafale.

Other important aircraft of the contemporary era are refueling aircraft such as the Boeing KC-767, and its future descendent the KC-46, as well as the Airbus A330 MRTT, or the new radar planes, such as the Boeing E-767 and E-8, the Boeing 737 AEW&C, the Embraer EMB145 AEW&C and the Gulfstream G.550 CAEW. There are also maritime patrol craft such as the Boeing P-8 Poseidon, the

ATR-42/72MP and the CASA C235MP and 295MP, and the new European transport aircraft the Airbus Military A400M, the Italian Alenia Aermacchi C-27J and the American Boeing C-17 Globemaster III, not forgetting the latest generation trainers, such as the Alenia Aermacchi M-346 and the Kai T-50, as well as the revolutionary convertiplanes, the military Bell Boeing V-22 Osprey and the civilian AgustaWestland AW.609.

60
This is the prototype of the CASA-EADS
C-295 AEW.

60-61
The most modern American military
transport aircraft is the Boeing C-17.

Chapter 4

FOR WORK AND FOR PLAY:
CIVIL AIRCRAFT

CIVIL AND COMMERCIAL AIR TRANSPORT IS ONE OF THOSE AREAS OF THE WORLD ECONOMY WHICH, OVER THE LAST 40 YEARS, HAVE SEEN AN EVER-LARGER AND MORE DIZZYING DEVELOPMENT.

THE AGE OF THE GREAT PLANES WAS OPENED BY THE BOEING 707 AND THE DOUGLAS DC-8, TWO PLANES THAT MADE THEIR APPEARANCE IN THE 1950S. BUT THE BOEING 747, THE "JUMBO JET," WHICH MADE ITS FIRST FLIGHT IN 1969, WAS THE FIRST PLANE OF THE MODERN AGE, AND THE FIRST WIDE-BODY, INTRODUCING PASSENGER DECKS OVER TWO LEVELS, A HUGE SIZE FOR THE TIME, AND AN UNPRECEDENTED TRANSPORT CAPACITY, ACCOMMODATING ALMOST 400 PASSENGERS IN THE STANDARD CONFIGURATION. WITH ITS EXCEPTIONAL CHARACTERISTICS, THE JUMBO CREATED VARIOUS PROBLEMS, ESPECIALLY REGARDING ITS LARGE SIZE AND THE MANAGEMENT OF ITS PASSENGERS AND THEIR LUGGAGE IN AIRPORTS WHICH HAD TO GEAR UP TO MEET THE NEW NEEDS.

62
The Boeing 747 Jumbo Jet was the first wide-body transport plane.
It appeared in 1969, and could hold on average 400 passengers.

A contemporary of the jumbo was another aircraft that wrote the history of aviation, the Franco-British Concorde, the first and, as of today, only supersonic passenger aircraft. This plane also flew for the first time in 1969, but the philosophy behind its construction was the absolute opposite of that of the 747. This aircraft in fact was intended to offer passengers not a large number of seats or a certain level of comfort, but pure speed, given that it

was capable of cruising at mach 2, more than 1,242 mph (2,000 km/h approx). The program was very expensive, and required the agreement of the governments of France and Great Britain to make it a reality. Despite the pride of the countries that built it and the technical success of the aircraft, the Concorde proved to be too noisy for many airports, and above all too expensive to buy and keep in service; it was used only by the French and British national companies.

Its end began on July 25, 2000 when an Air France Concorde crashed shortly after takeoff: all 109 people aboard were killed, along with four on the ground.

The aircraft was officially withdrawn on November 26, 2003.

64
A Lufthansa Boeing 747 taking off. More than 1450 of this plane have been built and it is still in production.

64-65
The fastest and most elegant passenger jet plane in history was the Anglo-French Concorde, which cruised at Mach 2.

66
The first of the successful Airbus family was the A300.

67
One of the smallest airplanes of the Airbus A300/320 family is the 319.

The future of air transport was destined to develop as the result of a struggle between two industrial giants: Airbus and Boeing. In 1970, Europe had finally managed to give birth to a multinational consortium able to match the large American industries. Airbus Industrie was born, in fact, from the desire of France, Germany and Great Britain to give life to a new twin-engined wide-body aircraft for short and medium range with innovative features, capable of breaking the American monopoly. This aircraft, the planning of which was begun in 1967, was named the Airbus A300 and first flew in 1972, before entering service with Air France in 1974. The project had been carefully planned to be developed in modules, giving rise to larger or smaller aircraft, depending on the needs of the airlines and markets. Thus in 1982 appeared the A310 model, with a short body, but with a new wing design, while 1993 saw the appearance of the A321 with a stretched fuselage, and 1995 the A319, the shortest of the family.

At the end of the 1980s, Airbus decided to increase its range by also building long-haul aircraft. In 1987 the A330/A340 model was launched, which differed mainly in its use of two or four (A330) engines. These aircraft were able to carry 250-350 passengers (depending on their configuration) for distances of about 11,000 kilometers. The next move from Airbus was to focus on the construction of the largest aircraft in the history of civil aviation. The A380 was begun in 2000 and its first flight took place in 2005. The basic model of the A380-800 has a maximum takeoff weight of over 550 tons and can accommodate up to a maximum of 850 passengers on two levels. Despite some initial difficulties, the A380 entered service in 2007, but, as could be expected, its production numbers are much lower than those of conventional aircraft.

68-69
In 2005 Airbus launched the world's biggest passenger plane, the A380, which can carry up to 850 passengers.

Faced by the success of Airbus, on the other side of the ocean, American industry was not resting on its laurels. Boeing, the only large U.S. company that remained in the field of passenger aircraft, had launched projects in the 1970s for two newly conceived aircraft, which were intended to maintain their supremacy over the European manufacturer. The first of these was the B767, which made its first flight in September 1981. Conceptually, this aircraft was quite similar to the A300, employing two engines and very similar aerodynamics, while the number of seats ranged between 180 and 224. This model, which was intended primarily for long-range flights, was developed in several versions, the last of which is the 767-400ER, an aircraft that can carry 290 passengers over distances of more than 6,835 miles (11,000 km), and which came into service in 2000. Almost contemporary with the 767 was the B757, which first flew in 1982, placing itself immediately in competition with the A300. The 757 very much recalled its big brother the 767, and could carry between 150 and 180 pas-

sengers, depending on the configuration chosen by the airlines. This aircraft was a sales success, but at the beginning of the twenty-first century, the market began to prefer smaller aircraft, and production of the B757 ended in 2004, after having reached a total of 1,050 units built.

The successor to this aircraft was, on the basis of the preferences of the airlines, the Boeing 737NG (Next Generation), an aircraft launched in the nineties to face the direct competition of the Airbus A319/320/321. The first of the new 737s, the 737-700, took off in 1997.

70-71
The Boeing 737 family is as enduring as it is efficient. This is a photograph of the 737-800 model, which appeared in 1997.

To compete with Airbus on all fronts, in 1986 Boeing launched the 777, a large long-haul aircraft, meant to compete with the A330/340 and replace the B767 and the older B747. The new aircraft flew in 1994, and was the first Boeing with fly-by-wire flight controls, and fully designed on computers. The 777-300 model is the largest twin-jet plane in the world, and can carry from 350 to 550 passengers. Boeing's most modern aircraft is now the Boeing 787 Dreamliner, which flew for the first time in 2009. This model is the most advanced American industry can offer, and is characterized by high-efficiency engines and wings, 80% constructed of composite materials, a cockpit with large LCD screens, head-up displays for the pilots, and other latest generation technical devices. The passengers on board, in a typical configuration, number about 240, and it has a range of over 9,320 miles (15,000 km). The first aircraft entered service in 2011 with All Nippon Airways.

72-73
The Boeing 777 took off in 1994 for long-range flights. It is the biggest twinjet in the world.

After the 1970s, private flying did not experience a period of expansion, and the aircraft used by flying clubs have remained largely the same, but with the introduction of a few new aircraft, such as the SOCATA TB-9 and TB-10, which continued the success of French production, which was already

established with the Robin 400 and Morane-Saulnier Rallye, and that of the Italians, who had made the SIAI Marchetti S.205/208 and Partenavia P.66. There had also been considerable development in aircraft for aerobatics competitions, with increasingly sophisticated models, such as the Zlin 50 and 242, the Yak-50 and 55, the Sukhoi Su-26 and 29, and the CAP 10, 20 and 230 series.

74
The TB-10 Tobago is, one of the three most
successful private aircraft by SOCATA.

74-75
The single-engine Robin DR400 is a
characteristic French private plane.

76-77
The Dassault Falcon intercontinental
7X model.

77
A twinjet in flight.

However, in recent times the industry has suffered, especially in Europe, because of high costs and cumbersome bureaucracy. There has thus been a gradual growth in the ultralight sector, simpler aircraft subject to fewer regulatory restrictions. These aircraft are manufactured by many companies all over the world in hundreds of different

models, have affordable starting prices and in some cases have achieved remarkable levels of sophistication in construction, such as the Italian Blackshape Prime. In Italy, models that have achieved great success are the Savannah and Tecnam P92 while internationally there are the Lazair, the Savage, the Quicksilver MX Sprint, the Kolb FireStar, the tiny twin-engine Cri-Cri, and many, many others. In the field of business aircraft too, or business jets, many models have become established, such as the Dassault Falcon family, Gulfstream and Learjet.

INDEX

PHOTO CREDITS

Bettmann/Corbis: pages 4, 16-17

De Agostini Picture Library: pages 1, 12-13, 13 top, 13 bottom, 14, 15, 18, 19, 20-21, 26-27, 27, 29, 32-33, 34 top, 36, 37, 40-41, 41 bottom, 41 top, 42-43, 42 top, 42 bottom, 55, 66, 74, 74-75

Sander de Haas/iStockphoto: pages 62, 64-65, 67

Leemage/Universal Images Group/Getty Images Group: page 17

Library of Congress/Digital version by Science Faction/Getty Images: pages 10-11

Riccardo Niccoli: pages 5, 6-7, 8-9, 22-23, 24, 28-29, 30, 30-31, 34 bottom, 35, 38-39, 39, 44, 46, 47, 48, 48-49, 50, 51, 52-53, 53, 54-55, 56-57, 58, 58-59, 60, 60-61, 64, 68-69, 70-71, 72-73, 76-77

Shutterstock: pages 2-3

Stephen Strathoke/iStockphoto: page 77

Cover: Pitts Special acrobatic biplane.
Tyson Rininger/Check Six/Getty Images
Back cover: A formation of F-117s in flight.
Riccardo Niccoli

AUTHOR

Riccardo Niccoli, a journalist, writer, photographer, and one of Italy's best-known aeronautical historians, has written on the subject in specialized magazines since 1982. A graduate in political science, he writes for many publishers in Europe and the United States, and is the author of various books on aeronautical subjects. He is the author of *The Great Book of Combat Aircraft*, White Star Publishers.

WS White Star Publishers® is a registered trademark
property of De Agostini Libri S.p.A.

© 2013 De Agostini Libri S.p.A.
Via G. da Verrazano, 15
28100 Novara, Italy
www.whitestar.it - www.deagostini.it

Translation: Contextus s.r.l., Pavia (Martin Maguire)
Editing: Contextus s.r.l., Pavia

ISBN 978-88-544-0801-2
1 2 3 4 5 6   17 16 15 14 13

Printed in China